# RESET

## BY NICK HALL

## #JesusChangesEverything

RESET *Study Guide*
© 2016 by Outreach, Inc.

Published by Outreach, Inc., Colorado Springs, CO 80919
www.Outreach.com

ISBN: 9781942027461
Cover Design by Tim Downs
Interior Design by Alexia Garaventa
Written by Nick Hall
Edited by Tia Smith

Printed in the United States of America

# CONTENTS

# INTRODUCTION

# WHAT TO KNOW BEFORE YOU DIVE IN

Welcome to the *Reset Study Guide*. Whether you're a long-time small-group veteran or this is your first group experience, you are in for four inspiring and life-giving meetings as you and a handful of others consider what a "reset" might look like for you.

To reset something is, literally, to set it back to its original purpose, its original design. When a phone, computer game, or DVR is functioning in a less-than-optimal way, you can *reset* it so that whatever was stuck gets unstuck and all the connections run smoothly again. Similarly—and perhaps astoundingly to you—when your life is functioning in a less-than-optimal way, *you can reset it too*. And in the same way that your piece of technology starts humming along once it has been reset, your life will start humming along as well.

This reset happens first on the inside, where our deep-seated cravings for significance and satisfaction live. That part of you that longs for fulfillment, the part that sometimes asks, "Is this all there is in life?"—*that's* the part that leads the charge in the reset of a human soul. Should you choose to accept Jesus's invitation to such a reset, you'll quickly find that there is much more to this life than you ever imagined.

The life Jesus promises to those who are reset by him is one of *abundance*, John 10:10 says, one that exceeds our every expectation. In Jesus, there is enough—enough forgiveness, enough grace, enough acceptance, enough love, enough confidence, enough resources, enough excitement, enough enjoyment, enough elation, enough peace. This series has been designed for the sole purpose of pointing you toward that enoughness.

You can be fulfilled. You can be reset. You can be changed—because Jesus changes everything.

## THE FOUR SESSIONS

Your small group will meet once a week for all four weeks of this series, and during each meeting, you will discuss one aspect of life that Jesus longs to reset. The four topics were derived from thousands upon thousands of emails from, text messages from, and in-person conversations held with participants who attended PULSE events over the past decade in every major city in the country. (For more on my ministry, PULSE, see page 92 in this guide.) The sessions are as follows:

- Week 1: "Jesus, Reset My Heart"—my faith, my belief system, the core of who I am

- Week 2: "Jesus, Reset My Mind"—the thoughts I entertain, the things I say to myself, my assumptions about my world

- Week 3: "Jesus, Reset My Voice"—what I say, how I say it, why I say it, and the role spiritual conversations play in my life

- Week 4: "Jesus, Reset My Hands"—how I choose to invest my time, talents, energies, and other resources day by day

# STUDY GUIDE ELEMENTS

To help you work through each week's content, the sessions have been divided into eight sections. They include:

## KEY SCRIPTURE

This is the main Bible passage that forms the spine of thought for the entire session. You'll notice that the New International Version is the primary translation cited throughout this guide, but your group leader may prefer to introduce additional translations as you go.

## CORE TRUTH

The Core Truth is a one- or two-sentence summary of that week's lesson.

## VIDEO NOTES

A two-page layout is provided for you to take notes each week, complete with prompts from that week's video clip.

## STUDY IT

The Study It section will help you dig into a Bible story or thoughtful position on the topic at hand. You and your group members will be asked to read the paragraphs in this section aloud each week.

## APPLY IT

Here, you will be invited to apply the principles from the Study It section to everyday life. As with the previous section, you will be asked to read this content aloud during group time.

## DISCUSS IT

During the Discuss It section, you will be given time and space to talk about your thoughts on and reactions to the subject that has been raised. A handful of questions are provided to spur on discussion, but your group leader has been instructed to adjust them based on your group's needs and interests.

## THE INVITATION TO RESET

At the conclusion of each session is The Invitation to Reset, a plea for you to trust Jesus in that week's aspect of life. (Hint: You won't ever regret saying "yes" to these invitations!)

## CLOSING PRAYER

A brief closing prayer is provided for your group each week.

# GROUP-TIME PREP

Prior to your group meetings, feel free to preview that week's session, focusing on the Key Scripture, the Core Truth, and the Discuss It questions that will be asked. If your church has decided to distribute Nick Hall's book *Reset: Jesus Changes Everything*, then you may wish to read that content prior to your first meeting as a way to orient your mind and heart to the subjects at hand.

Other ways to maximize your group experience include the following preparations:

- **Pray.** Pray for your group leader, for the other members of your group, and for your own heart to be pliable to what God wishes to do in and through you each week.

- **Plan.** As much as you're able, build some margin into your schedule on small-group days so that you can arrive on time (or even early) and unstressed. During the group meeting itself, work to stay focused on the discussion at hand instead of letting the obligations of your week overtake your thoughts.

- **Process.** Between group meetings, review your impressions from the previous week. Was God trying to get your attention in a particular area? If so, carve out time to think through that prompting and take action accordingly.

## A HEALTHY GIVE-AND-TAKE

As your group settles into a rhythm, you'll notice unique dynamics emerge. It may include talkers, quiet types, administrative masterminds, relational assimilators, conversational geniuses, justice-seekers, antagonists, optimists, pessimists, those who love Jesus, and perhaps a few who do not. It's important to realize that groups of *all* shapes, sizes, and make-ups have the potential to be wonderful laboratories where great spiritual growth and development can occur as long as its members are engaged, accepting, respectful, and willing to learn. The encouragement here, of course, is that you choose to be one such member.

Be mindful of others' styles, and work to adjust your style accordingly. If you are highly extroverted, you think quickly on your feet, you always have an opinion, and you are completely comfortable sharing your thoughts in a group setting, then you will do well to remember those who are less confident and comfortable and enfold them in discussion as you're able. Likewise, if you are one of the quieter ones, be mindful that not everyone has to be "drawn out" in order to share their thoughts and be willing to take the initiative from time to time and ask for the floor.

If you notice a group dynamic that you believe is inhibiting your group's ability to thrive, ask your leader for ideas on how to resolve the issue.

## READY, SET, *RESET*

As you get started, know that scores of people have been praying specifically for *you,* that you would delight in this material and that, ultimately, the reset Jesus wants to provide you would be welcomed in your life.

# "JESUS, RESET MY HEART"

## *IT ALL STARTS HERE*

## KEY SCRIPTURE

*[Have someone in your group read these verses and the following Core Truth aloud before playing this week's video.]*

"Who may ascend the mountain of the LORD? Who may stand in his holy place? The one who has clean hands and a pure heart, who does not trust in an idol or swear by a false god." — Psalm 24:3–4

## CORE TRUTH

The reset that Jesus offers begins with you and me. When we allow our lives to be reset from sin, cynicism, and self-reliance to faith in Jesus—his grace, his love, his transformation—all the other resets we want and need can and will follow.

# VIDEO NOTES

*[Play this week's video and then take turns in your group reading the Study It paragraphs aloud.]*

## PSALM 24:3–4

_____

_____

_____

_____

_____

_____

_____

## THE BEGINNING OF A MOVEMENT

_____

_____

_____

_____

_____

_____

_____

## JAZER'S STORY

_____

_____

_____

_____

_____

_____

_____

## FAITH AS A NECESSARY FIRST STEP

_____

_____

_____

_____

_____

_____

## A RESET HEART, A BRAND-NEW HEART

_____

_____

_____

_____

_____

_____

_____

# STUDY IT

Right now, you are putting your faith in something. We all are. Moment by moment, circumstance by circumstance, crisis by crisis, we look to someone or something to address the ache deep inside of us, the throbbing sensation that this life we're living isn't at all what we signed up for, not *at all* what we hoped it would be. And so while my "someone or something" might be different from your "someone or something," we're both looking *somewhere* to ease that pain.

I've been talking to people for twenty years about the direct objects of their faith, and those things span a vast ocean of space. People put their faith in their spouse, in their bank account, in their kids' success, or in their job. They put their faith in stock-market futures, in today's well-crafted to-do list, or in "the way things have always been." While the responses are as diverse, almost all of them boil down to this simple fact: *They put their faith in themselves.*

Most of us are trained from the youngest of ages to do things all by ourselves. My wife and I have two young children, and it seems we praise them each and every time they learn to achieve something without our assistance (especially as it pertains to bathroom duties). For example (I'll stay away from those potty examples . . . you're welcome), when Truett first put a spoonful of food to his lips without my wife, Tiffany, directing the utensil for him, he smiled and repeated what we'd been cheering him toward for weeks: "I do it all-by-'self, Mommy!"

All-by-'self seems like a harmless goal, and coming from our toddler, it is pretty cute. But for those of us who (hopefully) have left childishness behind and are straining toward being fully formed, fully functioning, even godly influencers in the world today, our leaning toward independence can be deadly.

## THANKS BUT NO, THANKS

When I talk with people about shifting their faith from self-reliance to reliance on Jesus, one of two responses typically surfaces, the first being doubt or downright dissent. As I wrote in my book *Reset: Jesus Changes Everything,* if faith is defined as "confidence in what we hope for and assurance about what we do not see" (Hebrews 11:1), their reaction runs along the lines of,

> *Confidence in what we hope for? Nah, we'd*
>
> *rather place confidence in where we've*
>
> *been, what we've already done, what is*
>
> *real, what is known. Assurance about what*
>
> *we do not see? No, thanks. We're only sure*
>
> *about what our five senses detect.*[1]

Most of us have been trying and striving for so long that it can seem impossible to let go. We trust our strength, our ideas, and our ability to outwit, outplay, and outlast everyone else on the island so deeply that we honestly have no idea how to loosen the grip on the controls of life. Even an offer from a loving God to bear the stress of sorting out our lives and lead us into a better, brighter future isn't enough. So while "let go and let God" may work for our friends who've been through AA, it's only because they simply don't have the "strength" we do to make it on our own.

## I GET IT. REALLY, I DO.

Even though my greatest passion, my surest mission, and my very living all center on promoting this move from faith in self to faith in Jesus, I totally get why people refuse to believe that such a shift is right for them. Think about it: People who make life-altering decisions (or *any* decisions, really) based on nebulous, squishy, unseen "faith stuff" can seem a little . . . *off*. The story of one famous Bible character in particular comes to mind, a man I call Warren in my book. Check out the following setup; any guesses as to who we're talking about?

> *Imagine some seventy-five-year-old man—*
>
> *we'll call him Warren—who suddenly*
>
> *started having visions. He couldn't explain*
>
> *what was happening. Was his wife trying*
>
> *some new ingredients in her beef casserole?*
>
> *Had he been getting enough sleep? Soon*
>
> *after the visions came, a voice said to him,*
>
> *"Leave everything. Pack what you can. Grab*
>
> *your family, and hit the road. I will give you*
>
> *directions later."*

*Can you imagine if Warren was your uncle or grandfather and called to give you the news that he was going to ditch all his earthly possessions—his home, his car, his sweet La-Z-Boy recliner—and head off to who knows where and possibly live there for the rest of his life? I think most of us would think it was time to put Uncle Warren in a nursing home.*[2]

The story comes from Genesis 12 and centers on Abram (soon to be renamed Abraham by God), the guy we Christians consider the "father of our faith." During what should have been his retirement years—you know, when people spend their days lazing around on the beach perfecting that imitation-leather tan, playing eighteen holes of golf five days a week, or straining for hours to hear their bingo numbers called night after night—God whispered a quick directive into Abram's ear: "Pack up, my friend. Get up. Go. I'll provide more details as things unfold."

Now, I don't know about you, but if I were on the receiving end of that whisper, despite how I feel about Jesus and what I firmly believe about faith, my first response would be something like, "Huh? Really? Wait, *what?*"

I'm not sure why this is true, but whenever even the most faithful follower of Jesus is invited into an adventure with him, the natural human reaction is to see the proposition through the lens of rational convention rather than divine intervention. We want *wise* input, input that makes *sense* to us, input that can be substantiated by scientific fact or dependable polls, by trustworthy friends, or at *least* by the latest trends. I mean, if you were just cruising along, doing fine, feeling good, enjoying life, and God asked *you* to pick up stakes and move to a new place (which will be disclosed later), what would you do? Would you eye the heavens skeptically, as though surely you'd heard things wrong, or would you exhale the familiarity of your current life, open your palms toward God, and say, "If this is you, I'm in. You lead, and I'll follow. You say the word, and I'll go."

If you'd hesitate even for a moment, don't feel bad; most of us shortsighted, fallible human beings would too. But if there is even a hint of curiosity in you about what that "ready yes" response to God would look like, the Bible offers plenty of examples of men and women who lived it out. And lest I spoil their stories' endings for you, I'll leave it at this: Things turned out pretty good.

## IN SEARCH OF A "READY YES"

At its core, the problem with relying on our own strength and ability is that at some point they will fail us, leaving us with little more than disillusionment and pain. When we're left feeling disillusioned and in pain, we feel terrible, and because we don't like feeling terrible, we will seek out ways to make those terrible feelings go away. We turn to substances, such as drugs, meds, alcohol, cigarettes, and food. We turn to video games, movies, or porn—anything to help us escape from the reality we face. We turn to partying, shopping, busyness, workaholism, exercise, fads. We turn to anything, really, that promises distraction from the agony that is "real life." This is the trouble with self-reliance; it leads us nowhere good. It's only when we surrender that control to the One who made us, loves us, and promises to sustain us that we'll find life that is truly life.

This brings me to the second response I hear from people when I encourage them to go Jesus's way. Rather than doubt his existence, his sufficiency, or his grace, they trust that he is who he says he is and that he will do what he says he will do. They step toward Jesus—admittedly tiny baby steps at first—resolved to take him at his word.

I call this the "ready yes," a clear sign of blooming faith in a person's heart.

A "ready yes" means that whenever God calls, you pick up. Whenever he reaches out, you're available. Whenever he whispers, you lean in. Whenever he invites you into an adventure, instead of glancing skeptically toward heaven, waiting for substantiation, or trolling for friends' approval, *you readily, wholeheartedly say "yes."*

Hebrews 11 is stuffed full with people who wasted no time saying "yes" to God (think: Abel, Enoch, Sarah, Moses, Rahab, Gideon, and Samson), and according to the opening verses, they were commended by him as a result. Now, I fully acknowledge how exciting it feels to get commended by our colleagues, by our Twitter and Instagram followers, by our Facebook friends, by our family members, and by the watching world. Who doesn't love the atta-boy or atta-girl, the praise, the "like," the reward? It feels so good when someone notices us and tells us how awesome we are. But here's another thing I know: *It's going to feel exponentially better when that commendation comes from God.*

In this week's video, you were introduced to my buddy Jazer, a young man whose story proves the power of shifting from faith-in-self to faith-in-Jesus. I have to tell you, every time I think about Jazer's journey, I can't help but grin a goofy grin. The guy was headed for outright self-destruction—as we all are when we rely on ourselves. But then, enter *Jesus.* An invitation to trust Him, a willing heart ready to submit, acceptance from the Lover of souls, grateful tears, and a "ready yes."

Today, right this minute as I write this, Jazer is on a bus, in a car, or on a plane, traveling all over the country to challenge and rally students for Jesus. He helped us lead the grassroots effort toward Together 2016, encouraging his generation to rally together for a worthwhile cause. He always challenges students to pray and encourages them to renew their faith when it has grown ineffective and jaded.

If you had told him a few years ago that this is where he would be today, I think he would have laughed at you. "Traveling for Jesus? For *my* life? Are you *insane?*" And yet that's exactly what has transpired for him. Jesus—One and Only—has moved in. Jazer, as a result, found his "ready yes"—the "yes" reserved for God alone. Because of that unabashed "yes," Jazer is aiming for a life that is bound to net some pretty cool words one day. I believe he can keep going and finish strong because Jesus is in him. And on the day his earthly life ends and entrance to heaven is celebrated and secured, I believe the words that will resound throughout the kingdom will be, "Well done, good and faithful servant. Your Father is so pleased."

## DOUBTER OR DEVOTEE?

The obvious question that remains here centers on which you will choose to be: dissenting doubter or faithful devotee. In the next section, we'll walk through the simple progression that helped me when I was wrestling with the claims of Christ. But for now, let me encourage you with these words from *Reset:*

> *If you are tired of living for nothing more than your hopes, your dreams, your desires, and your needs, and you want to start living beyond yourself, Jesus stands ready to reset your faith. If you are bored from praying prayers that you can manage on your own and want to start boldly petitioning all of heaven to radically change your world, Jesus stands ready to reset your faith. . . . If you've grown cynical about whether God still lives and moves and breathes in and through his people, whether there are still miracles in our midst, whether your life is destined for*

*more than a lackluster existence that tragi-*

*cally resembles a gerbil running his scrawny*

*legs ragged on a wheel going nowhere fast,*

*Jesus stands ready to reset your faith.*[3]

It all begins here—with you saying "yes" to him; at the core of the reset all we need in life is a surrender to the only One worthy of our trust. Listen, if I were a betting man, I'd wager that once you allowed Jesus to reset your faith, to reset your entire life, you'd stand *forever* by the choice you made.

## APPLY IT

*[Have one member of your group read the following section aloud as a prelude to the Discuss It questions.]*

When I was a small child—only three or four years old—I started asking questions about God. Between pestering my mom and dad about why my sister was so giggly all the time, whether I could stay up late that night, and how long they thought it would take me to make the roster for the Minnesota Twins, I wanted to know about God. Specifically, I needed to know where people went when they died, and so patiently, lovingly, and frequently, one or both of my parents would disclose to me the great mysteries of life and death and life after death in terms that a preschooler could grasp.

From that age forward, I made it my habit to ask anyone and everyone I stumbled upon whether they knew Jesus and loved Jesus and thus were going to heaven when they died. I was a passionate little evangelist, daily thrusting very deep, very personal questions on unsuspecting grown-ups and kids alike. I loved what I knew of Jesus and wanted everyone else to love him too.

My faith hit a rough patch during my teenage years as I started to struggle with purity. I had accidentally seen some inappropriate pictures of women years prior and between locker-room jokes and images popping up on my screen, I got hooked. What I couldn't have known is that what began as (relatively) innocent curiosity would spread like wildfire in my mind and heart, and the ultimate burn scar from that habit would affect every nook and cranny of my life.

While I was battling to overcome that sin, something that had previously felt very alive in me was starting to die. In hindsight I can see that the issue was this: I was turning to relationships and lust because I wasn't finding satisfaction in its proper place. I was trying to fulfill the needs and desires God placed inside me in ways that directly dishonored him, and I was miserable as a result. If I ever hoped to rekindle the spark for Jesus I'd had as a young boy, I was going to have to find a way to put into practice what I'd only known in theory before. I was going to have to invite Jesus to reset my purity . . . by resetting my faith in him first.

I decided the best place to start was with an honest conversation with God. If I recall, it went something like this: "God, I'm sorry. This isn't who I am. It isn't who I want to be. I'm tired of trying to find satisfaction everywhere else. I need you. Please help me."

From there, I followed the simple exhortations of Scripture I'd memorized years prior: "Come to me," Jesus said. "Consider the fact that because I won victory over death and sin, I can win victory over the trials and setbacks you face." "Walk with me all your days." And so I did just that: I came. I considered. I stayed close. And little by little, my struggle with purity and porn was replaced by affection and allegiance for Jesus.

If you are looking for practical ways to initiate faith-fueled living—whether for the first time or the thousandth, whether you're stuck in a season of bondage or you're simply convinced there must be more to life—then maybe that progression will help you as much as it helped me.

## COME

In Matthew 11:28, Jesus said, "Come to me, all you who are weary and burdened, and I will give you rest." If you have been bearing the brunt of planning, controlling, and orchestrating your days and are ready to let God take his rightful place as the leader of your life, then the first step to take is simply to come.

You, whoever you are and wherever you've been, *come*. Come to Jesus. Come, and he will give you rest.

## CONSIDER

As you enter the presence of Christ, consider his claims afresh. In various places in Scripture, he confirms that he is God's Son—fully God and fully man—and that he is the one and only path leading from humankind to God. He says that he is the way, the truth, and the life. He says that he is love.

What is standing between you and Jesus right now? If you could ask the God of the universe for a supernatural reset for any area(s) of your life, what would it be? Take inventory of your life and be real before the God who made you for more. Peel back the superficial layers people down through the ages have tried to wrap around Jesus—that he is white, boring, anti-everything, and . . .

(fill in the blank)—and work to see Jesus as he is presented in Scripture. Start with these verses, and see where you are led from there: John 4:13–14, John 10:10–11, John 14:6, Matthew 6:33, Mark 8:34–37, and Mark 10:45.

Consider Jesus for who *he* says he is. And consider what's standing between you and him. In 1 John 1:9, Jesus's beloved disciple said, "If we confess our sins, he is faithful and just and will forgive us our sins and purify us from all unrighteousness." Whatever needs to be reset in your life can be reset today. Simply pray something along these lines: "Jesus, please forgive me for the things I have been turning to instead of you. Forgive me for the sin in my life. Reset me. Reset my faith and allegiance to you. I believe you died on the cross for my sin and rose from the grave. Fill me with your Spirit and lead my life. In Jesus's name, amen."

## STAY CLOSE

Finally, once you come near to Jesus and consider his claims, *stay close*. Just as the best way to really understand a book is to talk with the person who wrote it, the best way to understand and practice faith is to meet frequently with the One who authored it. Hebrews 12:2 names Jesus as the "author and perfecter" (NASB) of our faith, which means that while it is our responsibility to stay close, it is *his* responsibility to grow and complete our faith.

We don't have to clean ourselves up, work our "stuff" out, or rack up extra points so that Jesus will be impressed. We simply have to turn toward him instead of turning away, minute by minute, hour by hour, day by day. In *Reset*, I capture the promise of John 10:10 this way:

> *"I came so they can have real and eternal*
>
> *life," [Jesus] says in John 10:10, "more and*
>
> *better life than they ever dreamed of." We*
>
> *think we know how to secure "more and*
>
> *better life" for ourselves. I certainly thought*
>
> *I knew back when I was chasing after sink-*
>
> *ing sand instead of Jesus. And I've talked*
>
> *with hundreds if not thousands of guys who*
>
> *have fallen into the very same trap. If I can*
>
> *just fill up on her texts, her words, her*
>
> *likes, her hips, her kiss, they think, then*
>
> *I'll be satisfied. Then I won't feel this*
>
> *deep ache. But of course that sort of filling*
>
> *up doesn't yield fulfillment in the end. At*
>
> *best, it's all a glimpse of something greater,*
>
> *an arrow pointing us back to God. At worst,*

*we are left exposed and alone . . . desper-*

*ate for someone to show us a better way.*

*Only Jesus fills us up in the end.*[4]

What I proved to myself, I'm confident you'll find true in your own life too: Standing on the Rock of Jesus beats the instability of sinking sand any day. The faith-in-Jesus life is the best life there is.

# DISCUSS IT

*[Work through as many of the following questions as group time and interest will allow.]*

1. What are you putting your faith in today? Which of the following ideas resonate most with you? Check all that apply.

   ○ My spouse

   ○ My bank account

   ○ My kids' success

   ○ My job

   ○ The stock market

   ○ My to-do list

   ○ The way things have always been

   ○ The way I wish things would be

   ○ Some habit

   ○ Something/someone else

   ○ Myself

   ○ Jesus

2. How well is your current approach serving you in daily life?

3. When you consider the idea of putting your faith more fully in Jesus, what doubts or concerns come to mind? What experiences or assumptions do you think fuel those reservations?

4. What is your reaction to Jazer's story? In your own life, when have you seen faith in Jesus dramatically affect a person's life or set of circumstances? What is your own experience, if any, with this type of dramatic faith encounter?

5. Which of the present challenges, obstacles, or setbacks in your life would you most hope Jesus would address if you were to begin relying on him instead of yourself to make things work? In other words, what would the "more and better life" referenced in John 10:10 (MSG) look like for you?

# THE INVITATION TO RESET

*[Allow time for your group to read the following invitation silently. Then, have a designated group member close your time in prayer.]*

A beautiful story from Mark 10 features a blind man, great faith, and a radical encounter with Jesus. Bartimaeus, the blind man, was sitting by the road, begging for change from passersby, when Jesus happened by. Having heard about Jesus's miracle-working power, he called out, "Jesus, Son of David, have mercy on me!" (verse 47). Some from the crowd that was surrounding Jesus tried to shush Bartimaeus, thinking that Jesus would want nothing to do with a blind beggar's harassment, but in response, Jesus shushed the shushers. "Call him," Jesus said, referring to Bartimaeus (verse 49). His disciples did as instructed, bringing the blind man right to Jesus.

With Bartimaeus now directly before him, Jesus said, "What do you want me to do for you?" to which the blind man said, "Rabbi [meaning teacher], I want to see" (verse 51). Jesus looked at the man who could not look back and said, "Go, . . . your faith has healed you" (verse 52), and the text tells us that immediately thereafter, as blind Bartimaeus made his way up the road, his sight was miraculously restored.

When Bartimaeus was faithful to *come*, he was divinely equipped to *go* in a healed state. This same invitation is extended to you today: Come to Jesus. Choose faith in him. Trust him to heal whatever it is you need healed. And then *go*. Continue on the path—whole and holy, healed and healthy, resolute in your belief that he makes a vastly better God than you do.

# CLOSING PRAYER

"Father, thank you for seeing us and knowing us, for accepting us and loving us. Thank you for making a way through your Son, Jesus, for our lives to be reset in full, and for lifting up in your Word the importance of starting with the reset of our faith. Give each one of us the courage to take the steps you are prompting us to take now as a result of this week's session. In Jesus's name we pray, amen."

# WEEK 2

# "JESUS, RESET MY MIND"

## *I AM WHAT I THINK ABOUT*

## KEY SCRIPTURE

*[Have someone in your group read this verse and the following Core Truth aloud before playing this week's video.]* "One thing I ask from the LORD, this only do I seek: that I may dwell in the house of the LORD all the days of my life, to gaze on the beauty of the LORD and to seek him in his temple." —Psalm 27:4

## CORE TRUTH

The best part of spending time with Jesus is that we get to know him. As we learn to focus on Jesus, we can't help but become more like him— more self-aware, more confident, more self-controlled, more content.

# VIDEO NOTES

*[Play this week's video and then take turns in your group reading the Study It paragraphs aloud.]*

## PSALM 27:4

_____

_____

_____

_____

_____

_____

_____

## THE THOUGHTS WE THINK

_____

_____

_____

_____

_____

_____

## THE MADMAN IN MARK 5

_____

_____

_____

_____

_____

_____

_____

## FOURTEEN HUNDRED FORTY MINUTES

_____

_____

_____

_____

_____

## WHERE TRANSFORMATION OCCURS

_____

_____

_____

_____

_____

_____

# STUDY IT

So, just out of curiosity, what *are* you thinking about right now?

And now?

And . . . now?

As you saw in this week's video, at any given moment, you and I are being assaulted by a barrage of thoughts that course through our minds and work to influence what we believe. Which begs the question, *What are you thinking about right now?*

It's more than a fun conversational icebreaker; without veering toward the melodramatic, it's a matter of life and death. Because what you're thinking about is eventually what you'll believe, and what you believe is exactly who you are.

## THE POWER OF A SINGLE THOUGHT

When guys and girls find me after a PULSE event to talk about how Jesus might factor into their lives, regardless of the unique specifics of their situation, what always underlies their struggles is a single, errant thought. It doesn't matter if the outward manifestation of their disbelief and discontent looks like drug abuse, alcohol abuse, self-harm, suicidal thoughts, anger, problems at school, rebellion against authority, obsessive-compulsive tendencies, binging, purging, perfectionism, detachment, apathy, or any of a thousand other things; what is always behind it all is a seemingly small but totally deadly lie:

*I'm not good enough.*

*I'm not smart enough.*

*I'm not thin enough.*

*I'm not strong enough.*

*I don't have what it takes.*

*I'll never have what it takes.*

*My life is pointless.*

*My life is worthless.*

*Nobody sees me.*

*Nobody values me.*

*Nobody cares.*

Somewhere along the way, one of these brief sentences floated into their brain, and without their knowing it, the words made themselves at home. Now, sometimes years and years later, the insidious idea that "I'm not enough" or "I'll never have what it takes" is so ingrained in their thinking, in their *person*, that to extricate it feels about as risky as surgically separating conjoined twins. In *Reset*, I wrote about a young man I met while on the road who personified this devastating dynamic. After a PULSE event, he walked up to me and handed me a crumpled piece of paper . . .

> *It was a letter from his dad about what a*
>
> *worthless human being he, the son, was.*
>
> *This kid had hung on to and read that let-*
>
> *ter every day for years. Those awful words*
>
> *from his father had defined who he was.*
>
> *He was held captive by hate. He began*
>
> *cutting because he deserved nothing more*

*than to be slashed and abused. He'd spent*

*his life screaming inside, pleading with*

*someone—anyone—for a way out.*[1]

Given the pervasiveness of the problem I'm talking about, there's a good chance you know exactly how this guy felt. At one point in your life or another, someone you cared about spoke words to you that cut you to the bone, or someone did something to you that conveyed hatred or worthlessness or disgust, and what you were left with was a flawed self-concept, the belief that you are somehow less-than as a human being.

The experience established a norm for you, which is that your value as a person is to be defined by external things—what others think, what others say, how others respond—and so as you continued on in life, you set about the task of finding approval to counterbalance the disapproval that was weighing you down.

## THE PURSUIT OF HAPPINESS

The problem with looking to other people to validate ourselves is that those other people are part of a vast societal system that is characterized by distraction, dissatisfaction, superficiality, and greed. I wrote in *Reset* that the latest research says we are exposed to upward of five thousand advertising images every single day,[2] which is a sobering number for sure. But it's not just the *quantity* of images that should trouble us; it's the quality of the messages they bear. Think about it: How many TV ads have *you* seen that tell you how wonderful you are, how beautiful you are, how smart you are, and how treasured you are? I can't think of any either.

The net effect of the advertising industry's "you aren't happy, but what we're selling you will make you happy" onslaught is that we're perpetually reminded that our early misgivings about ourselves—that we're not enough, that we're ugly or worthless or a burden to everyone we know—are actually *true*. And so we come away thinking, "Well, maybe those jeans really *will* help me feel better." And with that, the advertiser has won, and we have lost—in some cases, lost *big*. What we fail to remember each time we pursue something external in hopes of scratching our internal self-concept itch is that as soon as we drop fifty or a hundred bucks on those jeans that promise to make us finally feel good about ourselves, someone on Twitter or some hipster friend or some *other* clothing manufacturer will tell us that *those* jeans are no longer cool and that *their* jeans suddenly are. Try as we may, we will never be able to keep up with the latest car/clothes/travel destination/look/music scene/A-list crowd/beauty fix/sports stats/stock buy/"it" restaurant/desirable neighborhood/school-of-choice/hot author . . . Which is why, if we are defining ourselves according to our ability to be near these things, we will surely and ultimately prove our suspicions true, that we just can't make the cut.

One research psychologist, in a study focused on college co-eds, found that students who "based their self-worth on external sources—including appearance, approval from others and even their academic performance—reported more stress, anger, academic problems, relationship conflicts, and had higher levels of drug and alcohol use and symptoms of eating disorders."[3] To which I say, *of course* they did. When we evaluate ourselves according to what the world says is true of us and allow ourselves to turn over thoughts of inadequacy, insufficiency, incompetence, and ineptness in our minds as though they were hunks of slow-cooking meat on a rotisserie spit, it stands to reason that we'll come away angry, annoyed, and most likely looking for some substance to abuse. And since angry, annoyed, abuse-prone people tend to sin in immensely consequential ways, what we're dealing with here are high, high stakes.

This has certainly been true for me. Throughout my latter teenage years and in seasons of my adult life, I have struggled with feeling down and have discovered that depression runs in my family. If you think it's tough to assess yourself in light of what the world says is cool, it's even harder when you don't want to get out of bed. On these days, everyone around me seems happy, with perfect smiles, fulfilling relationships, exciting adventures, meaningful pursuits, and awesome hour-long workouts to boast about, while I lie there trying to find motivation. It has taken me years (and an amazing wife) to sort out a strategy for moving from darkness to light in these moments, but eventually, *light does break in.* I'd like to explain how that occurs.

## TWO KEY THINGS

Recently, the nonprofit Action for Happiness, in conjunction with the organization Do Something Different, asked five thousand people to rate themselves on ten habits that the latest scientific research revealed as being key to happiness.

The habits included giving (doing things for others), relating (connecting with people), appreciating (noticing the world around us), and resilience (finding ways to bounce back). Also on the list: *acceptance,* or being comfortable with who you are. The question asked, in particular, was this: "How often are you kind to yourself and think you're fine as you are?"[4] Based on what we've been talking about, it won't surprise you to learn that the average rating on a scale of one (never, not at all) to ten (always, all the time) was just barely above a five. In other words, when it comes to self-acceptance, at least as far as this survey was concerned, the general assessment people made of themselves was little more than a "Meh. Nothing special here."

One of the leaders of the survey, when asked to evaluate the results, said,

> Our society puts huge pressure on us to be successful and to constantly compare ourselves with others. This causes a great deal of unhappiness and anxiety. These findings remind us that if we can learn to be more accepting of ourselves as we really are, we're likely to be much happier. The results also confirm that our day-to-day habits have a much bigger impact on our happiness than we might imagine.[5]

This assessment is spot-on but impossible to implement on our own. It is important that we learn to accept ourselves—as we are, for who we are. And in order to do so, it is necessary that we scrutinize the rhythms of our days. These are the two key things that helped me learn to move through my depressive state into a more fulfilling, functional place: acceptance of self, by way of radically altered habits. Let's take them one at a time.

## ACCEPT YOURSELF AS GOD DOES

By the time I suffered my first bout of depression, I had been walking with God faithfully for several years. I had been practicing spiritual disciplines, such as prayer and reading the Bible, and so I was familiar—at least on some level—with "truth." I knew from Scripture, for instance, that according to God I was a "new creation" the moment I surrendered my life to Jesus (2 Corinthians 5:17) and that for anyone who trusted Jesus as Savior God has "rescued us from the dominion of darkness and brought us into the kingdom of the Son he loves" (Colossians 1:13). I knew that, as his child, he had installed in me a spirit not of fear and depression and angst, but "of power and of love and of a sound mind" (2 Timothy 1:7, NKJV). And I knew that whenever I felt my weakest, the surest way to feel strong again was to be empowered by the knowledge and glory of God (see 2 Peter 1:3–4). But knowing truth is different from being anchored by it.

Those promises never seemed personal to me until I hit that depressed state. In those moments, I had to choose to surrender to God's view of me. Like a girl I met at a PULSE event said after giving her life to Jesus, "I don't want to see myself the way the world sees me one minute longer. I want to start seeing myself the way God sees me." In my darkness, God's promises were a lifeline being tossed my way by a loving Father, saying, "Nick! Nick! Don't give in. Don't give up. I'm here. I'm near to you. I've got you, son. You can take me at my word!" While temptation always wants us to dive deeper into despair, God's Word is the anchor that can keep us above the water's edge.

The antidote to my depression? It has been *Scripture*, time and again. As I meditate on the words of Scripture, I come to life again. *I am new. I can be delivered from this. I am valued by God. I am a treasure of his. I am not destined for fear and depression. I am destined for life and strength. I am not defined by what I do but by what he did on the cross.* These words roll around in my brain and finally sink into my heart. And the dark thoughts are silenced by new thoughts, thoughts of hope and security and peace.

## THE ONLY HABIT YOU NEED

Now, you probably picked up on the fact that I never would have been able to move from those seasons of darkness into light had I not drawn on the truth of God's Word. What's more, I never would have been able to draw on the truth of God's Word had I not memorized key verses as a kid and to this day. And it's impossible to memorize key verses without opening a Bible, reading it, and deciding to take it to heart. I don't know how to say it more plainly than this: It was God's Word that rescued me when everyone and everything else had given up the search. God's Word came and found me in that terrifyingly dark and isolated place that no one else would dare to venture into. Of all the important things in life, there is no substitute for time with Jesus. And we spend time with Jesus by taking in his Word.

If you want to engage in a reset of your mind, you need to spend time reading, hearing, studying, memorizing, and immersing yourself in the Word of God. I mention numerous ways because all of us learn differently. I had a businessman recently tell me that he struggled to learn from Scripture until he joined a public reading group where they listen to chapters of the Bible together. Now, he listens to the Bible while reading it, and on the topic of internalizing Scripture he is one of the most passionate people I've ever met. No matter what method works for you, it's going to take time. Consistent time. Focused time. Prioritized time. But here is my guarantee for you: *Spend time experiencing the Bible, and your thought life will be made new.*

You were expecting something more complicated, I know. But it isn't more complicated than that. Crack open a Bible, or pull up an app on your phone. Read (or listen to) what it says. Take God at his Word. And prepare for the wild ride of having your thoughts shift from those that sound like self-hatred to ones that are centered on self-love.

Because I'm already on something of a research kick this week, let me give you another stat: According to the Gallup organization, a full 65 percent of Americans agree that the Bible answers "all or most of the basic questions of life."[6] This means that about two-thirds of us already believe that the problems we are facing (which all can be traced back—at least on some level—to our patterns of thought, remember?) are addressed in the pages of Scripture. Furthermore, based on the American Bible Society's findings, **88** percent of Americans have at least one Bible lying around their house.[7] On the surface, this all appears to be very good news. To sum up:

- We have feelings of inadequacy and insecurity that cause us to (a) think errantly about ourselves and (b) make poor emotional, relational, financial, and lifestyle choices as a result.

- To change those errant thoughts, we need an infusion of thoughts that are true.

- We (two-thirds of us, anyway) believe that the Bible is chock-full of true thoughts, thoughts that will help us successfully navigate the tough stuff of life.

- What do you know? Almost all of us own a Bible! (In some cases, four or five.)

And yet there's just one little thing missing here in our cheery progression: Despite our belief that the Bible's message is valid for daily living, and despite the reality that we most likely have a Bible sitting around, the vast benefits of Bible engagement only show up if we actually *engage*.

Here's my last stat for you: In 2014, a *Time* magazine study showed that while 143 million North Americans read their Facebook feeds every day, only 40 million read their Bible.[8] Don't read me wrong: I'm as enamored with social media as anyone and love the real-time, wide-spanning sense of connectedness it fosters. I'm simply proposing that we prioritize one habit above all the other stuff we do—checking posts, shopping online, watching *SportsCenter*, hanging out with friends, taking care of kids, cleaning the house, heading off to work, paying the bills, studying for tests, and more.

That one habit? The *Bible,* in *you.* Jesus said the wise build their house on the sturdiness and steadiness of the rock (see Matthew 7:24–27), which means the rebuild we're after has to start from the ground up.

# APPLY IT

*[Have one member of your group read the following section aloud as a prelude to the Discuss It questions.]*

The Bible, referring to itself, says that it is "truth" (John 17:17). That it is "God-breathed" and "useful for teaching, rebuking, correcting and training in righteousness," so that you and I will be "thoroughly equipped for every good work" (2 Timothy 3:16–17). That it is "alive and active" and "sharper than any double-edged sword," and that it "judges the thoughts and attitudes of the heart" (Hebrews 4:12). That it is a "lamp" for our feet and a "light" on our path (Psalm 119:105). That it "endures forever" (Isaiah 40:8). And that it was embodied in the person of Jesus as "the Word became flesh and made his dwelling among us . . . full of grace and truth" (John 1:14).

Ultimately, *this* is why we read the Father's Word, because this is how we come to know his Son. We come to the Bible in search of Jesus, the One who calms the chaos that plagues our thoughts.

## GET GOD'S WORD INTO YOUR MIND

And so, if you are ready for a reset in your thought life, the only habit you need is to get God's Word into your mind. Read it. Listen to it. Meditate on it. Memorize it. Believe it. Speak it. Live it. Choose a passage to meditate on from

Psalms or the Gospels (the books of Matthew, Mark, Luke, and John) that speaks to your specific situation, and then stand back as the power of Scripture starts to transform you from the inside out. As I said in *Reset*,

> *Whatever dark thoughts lurk in the recesses of your mind, convincing you that you're not smart, that you're not compassionate, that you're not important, that you're not enough—those beliefs can be silenced as we start taking God at his word and clinging to his promises for our life. The lies of hell cannot stand when we declare the name of Jesus. The truth about you is that you are created in the image of God to be holy and blameless before him. You were designed to have the mind of Christ and the peace of God pulsing through your veins. You were built to house the living God, the One who has overcome all things, including death itself. And that presence, the Holy Spirit of God, dwells inside you because of*

*Jesus's sacrifice on the cross. Your debt has*

*been paid in full.*[9]

Ditch the lies you've been believing, my friend. The truth is, you are *God's*—the crown of his creation, his treasure, his heartbeat, his friend.

## GET RESET, THOUGHT BY THOUGHT

Then, day by day, Bible-reading session by Bible-reading session, notice your thoughts being made new. This is what David—who penned Psalm 27, where this week's passage is taken from—must have understood: More than anything else we may want in this world, the one and only thing that will deliver on all the promises it makes is engagement with the living God. May we *dwell* with him. May we spend time *gazing* upon his beauty. May we *seek* him with everything we've got.

# DISCUSS IT

*[Work through as many of the following questions as group time and interest will allow.]*

1. What do you make of the comment from Lecrae that I mentioned in the video segment, that if we live for people's acceptance, we will die by their rejection? How have you experienced the temptation to define your self-worth by what other people think?

2. What types of thoughts tend to plague you most, and where do you believe they come from?

3. What have you turned to in the past, in an attempt to silence those thoughts? How effectively did those solutions work for you?

4. What is your posture toward the Bible today, and what assumptions, experiences, or other inputs have shaped it?

5. If God's Word could shine light in just one area of darkness you face today, what area would that be, and why?

# THE INVITATION TO RESET

*[Allow time for your group to read the following invitation silently. Then, have a designated group member close your time in prayer.]*

As I said in this week's video, just like that madman Jesus encountered in Mark 5, all of us have known what it is like to be locked up by feelings of worthlessness, weakness, the sense of exposure, and pain, yet those verses prove to us that even the most maddening experiences we have known are just one conversation with Jesus away from being subdued. The chaos can be calmed, and the Calmer is Jesus Christ.

If you need your mind reset today, pray the prayer that follows, silently, between you and God.

# CLOSING PRAYER

"Father, I need new thoughts. I am tired of being held captive by lies. Would you please draw me to your Word, to the specific books, chapters, and verses that I need to write on my mind, so that my thoughts can be reset? Teach me to treasure your Word. Prompt me to read it. Give me wisdom to understand it. And help me think differently from this day on. In Jesus's name, amen."

# "JESUS, RESET MY VOICE"

## *GOOD NEWS FOR BAD TIMES*

### KEY SCRIPTURE

*[Have someone in your group read these verses and the following Core Truth aloud before playing this week's video.]*

"My mouth will tell of your righteous deeds, of your saving acts all day long—though I know not how to relate them all. I will come and proclaim your mighty acts, Sovereign LORD; I will proclaim your righteous deeds, yours alone." —Psalm 71:15–16

### CORE TRUTH

Nothing is riskier than letting Jesus control our words, but nothing is more satisfying than speaking up for him.

# VIDEO NOTES

*[Play this week's video and then take turns in your group reading the Study It paragraphs aloud.]*

## PSALM 71:15–16

_____

_____

_____

_____

_____

_____

## THOSE THINGS WE TALK ABOUT

_____

_____

_____

_____

_____

## GINNA'S STORY

_____

_____

_____

## DAVID'S PLEA

## PEOPLE WHO NEED *YOUR* VOICE

# STUDY IT

Consider yourself warned. If you have engaged wholeheartedly in this study so far, meaning you have re-upped your faith in Jesus (or "upped" it to begin with, if you never had it before!) and are committed to writing God's Word on your mind and heart as the central priority of your days, then what's about to happen in your life is going to blow your mind. Because after your heart gets reset and your mind gets reset, what you're most likely in for is an all-out reset of your *voice*. How is this possible, you ask? Here's how: The words you speak start getting filtered through the light of the Scripture you are taking in day by day, and before you know it, you sound like a wiser, kinder, better version of yourself than the one you were before.

## BE LIKE MIKE

When I first started PULSE, a pastor in town reached out to me and told me that he had heard about me and about the ministry and wanted to know if there was any way he could support me in something of a mentorship role. He himself had started a ministry years prior and knew the unique challenges I would face. He believed in my calling and was clearly a man after God's own heart. This was an easy "yes."

What Mike didn't know was that for several weeks prior to receiving his phone call, I had been praying for God to direct me toward a mentor so that I could navigate the uncharted waters of PULSE's course with professionalism, wisdom, and grace. When we pray, God moves! At the time, I had no doubt Mike was that guy, but now, nearly a decade later, I can confirm that Mike most certainly *was* that guy.

He has become one of my closest friends and has kept my weary, sometimes-unwise self out of many a pitfall over the years. If I were to net out the unparalleled contribution this man has made in my life, I would sum it up this way: *He has used his words well.*

In his insightful prayers for me, in his heartfelt encouragement of me, in the astute questions he's lobbed my way, in his thoughtful voice mails, in his instructive emails, in his responses to my late-night "help me!" texts, Mike has stewarded every syllable in a manner I just know pleases God. If ever there were an exhibit A for what a reset voice looks and sounds like, Mike Montgomery is it. We would all do well to be like Mike.

I bring all of this up because out of all the things our world needs today, I believe God-honoring, light-bearing, hope-giving speech tops the list.

## WHAT THE WORLD NEEDS NOW

You don't need to be a news hound to know that the state of affairs in our world today is . . . shaky, to say the least. One click to the online source of your choice will tell you that today (like most any other day) is being overtaken by terrorism, homicide, suicide, genocide, political shenanigans, scandal, and greed. It's enough to depress even the eternal optimists in the crowd. Spend twenty minutes clicking through a few of these stories, and you'll have to peel yourself off the floor. "What is our world coming to?" you'll be left wondering. "Isn't there any good news to report?"

Now, listen. I'm not going to pretend that there is some easy answer to the admittedly complex issues plaguing our world today. But what I will stand by is this: We are not going to get anywhere useful as a society if we don't turn to Jesus and let him take over our words.

The Reverend Billy Graham is one of my all-time most respected heroes, and as it relates to the topic at hand, one of my favorite things about him is that you just can't find references to him having said negative things about others. Down through the decades, during his most intense speaking seasons reporters would try to pin him to one cause or another. They wanted him to speak out against issues or candidates or share his views on this or that. And do you know what Dr. Graham would say, each and every time? He'd say something like, "We all need a Savior, and that Savior is Jesus. I'm here to talk about Jesus."

*Bam.* How's *that* for a response?

No matter how hard they tried, they just couldn't get Billy Graham off-message. His message was Jesus, his passion was Jesus, his whole life was Jesus . . . and it's Jesus still today.

When I read the headlines, the singular thought that chases through my mind is right along those lines: "We need a Savior. We need Jesus."

The homicide statistics are not going to abate, apart from the power of Jesus.

The suicide rate is not going to plummet, apart from the power of Jesus.

Terrorism is not going to be defeated, apart from the power of Jesus.

On and on we could go with examples, but the answer would remain the same. Whatever threatens light and life and godliness today will simply *not be overcome* unless we draw on the strength of the One who defeated darkness, sin, and death.

## POWER IN THE NAME OF JESUS

Before we move into the practicalities of how to draw on Jesus's strength in hopes of pushing back the darkness we see and feel all around, let me take you on a quick trek of biblical substance regarding the power that is found in his name. As you read through the following litany (I've added emphasis to each), put a check beside the verses that spark special interest in your mind and heart. We'll come back to those selections later on.

- ○ "Salvation is found in no one else, for there is *no other name* under heaven given to mankind by which we must be saved." —Acts 4:12

- ○ "Therefore God exalted him to the highest place and gave him *the name that is above every name*, that at the name of Jesus every knee should bow, in heaven and on earth and under the earth, and every tongue acknowledge that Jesus Christ is Lord, to the glory of God the Father." —Philippians 2:9–11

- ○ "And I will do whatever you ask *in my name*, so that the Father may be glorified in the Son." —John 14:13

- ○ "The seventy-two [disciples] returned with joy and said, 'Lord, even the demons submit to us *in your name*.'" —Luke 10:17

- ○ "She will give birth to a son, and you are to give him *the name Jesus*, because he will save his people from their sins." —Matthew 1:21

○ "Or do you not know that wrongdoers will not in-herit the kingdom of God? Do not be deceived: Nei-ther the sexually immoral nor idolaters nor adul-terers nor men who have sex with men nor thieves nor the greedy nor drunkards nor slanderers nor swindlers will inherit the kingdom of God. And that is what some of you were. But you were washed, you were sanctified, you were justified *in the name of the Lord Jesus Christ* and by the Spirit of our God." —I Corinthians 6:9–11

○ "Everyone who calls on *the name of the Lord* will be saved." —Romans 10:13

○ "Peter replied, 'Repent and be baptized, every one of you, *in the name of Jesus Christ* for the forgiveness of your sins. And you will receive the gift of the Holy Spirit.'" —Acts 2:38

○ "And these signs will accompany those who believe: *In my name* they will drive out demons; they will speak in new tongues." —Mark 16:17

○ "No one is like you, LORD; you are great, and *your name* is mighty in power." —Jeremiah 10:6

○ "For to us a child is born, to us a son is given, and the government will be on his shoulders. And *he will be called* Wonderful Counselor, Mighty God, Everlasting Father, Prince of Peace." —Isaiah 9:6

○ "Then Peter said, 'Silver or gold I do not have, but what I do have I give you. *In the name of Jesus Christ of Nazareth*, walk.'" —Acts 3:6

○ "*The name of the* LORD *is a fortified tower; the righteous run to it and are safe.*" —Proverbs 18:10

○ "'*My name will be great* among the nations, from where the sun rises to where it sets. In every place incense and pure offerings will be brought to me, because *my name will be great* among the nations,' says the LORD Almighty." —Malachi 1:11

○ "Whoever believes in him is not condemned, but whoever does not believe stands condemned already because they have not believed *in the name of God's one and only Son.*" —John 3:18

○ "But the Advocate, the Holy Spirit, whom the Father will send *in my name*, will teach you all things and will remind you of everything I have said to you." —John 14:26

○ "I write these things to you who believe *in the name of the Son of God* so that you may know that you have eternal life." —1 John 5:13

○ "And now what are you waiting for? Get up, be baptized and wash your sins away, calling *on [Jesus's] name.*" —Acts 22:16

○ "You may ask me for anything *in my name*, and I will do it." —John 14:14

○ "Is anyone among you sick? Let them call the elders of the church to pray over them and anoint them with oil *in the name of the Lord.*" —James 5:14

○ "Therefore go and make disciples of all nations, baptizing them *in the name of the Father and of the Son and of the Holy Spirit.*" —Matthew 28:19

○ "All the prophets testify about him that everyone who believes in him receives forgiveness of sins *through his name.*" —Acts 10:43

"All hail the power of Jesus's name," we used to sing in my grandparents' church, and at my family's church today, we sing about how in that name there is power to "break every chain." This is such well-placed deference to Jesus's name because his is the most powerful name there is! But what does all of this have to do with our ability to have our minds blown by Jesus? And to build on the resets of faith and thought that we've experienced? And to have the words we speak begin to sound more like Jesus? And to be a beacon of light in an increasingly dark world? Let's take a look at those practicalities I mentioned earlier.

# APPLY IT

*[Have one member of your group read the following section aloud as a prelude to the Discuss It questions.]*

The resetting of our voice comes down to this simple fact: The more we are being genuinely led by faith in Jesus, the more we are compelled to know him—which is why Scripture reading becomes such an important discipline for us. Then, as we saturate our minds with his truth and start to see transformation having its way in our thought patterns, attitudes, and desires, we begin to communicate differently with the people we're around.

## OUR WORDS BRING PEACE

One of the ways our words start to sound different, as Jesus is allowed to reset our voice, is that they are fueled by the goal of *peace*. For example, instead of throwing up some hand gesture when a car cuts us off in traffic, we watch the driver fly past us and say, "Wow. They must be in a huge hurry. God, protect them as they go." Instead of getting defensive when our spouse asks why we're late getting home, we exhale, make eye contact, and say, "I'm really sorry. Please forgive me. Are you open to hearing what happened?" Instead of gossiping to a friend about your mutual friend's most recent questionable decision, when asked about it you simply say, "I'm sure she has her reasons . . ." and change the subject.

A reset voice is a voice of peace and reason that speaks tenderness, compassion, and wise words. A reset voice calls out the name of Jesus often.

## OUR WORDS BRING POWER

Only after we have established a peaceful communication environment can we make any headway toward meaningful spiritual dialogue. Why? Because nobody will have ears to hear what you want to say if you're in an irritated, angry, defensive, or aggressive state. Bring peace so that you can then bring power.

Bringing power to an acquaintance who mentions a recent struggle sounds like, "Can I pray for you real quick?"

Bringing power to a spouse who is stressed sounds like, "Jesus has gone before you in this. His presence will keep you from being overcome. Do you want to talk, or do you need some time alone?"

Bringing power to a colleague who begins to express interest not just in your professional life but also in your personal world sounds like, "I know we've never really talked about anything spiritual, but if you're open to it, I'd like to tell you about the journey I've been on with Jesus . . ."

Bringing power to a family member who is wrestling with whether God even exists sounds like, "Jesus loves you so much. He sees you and cares about you. He wants you to know him—not the caricatures of him, but really, truly *him*."

Bringing power to a friend who is embarrassed to tell you that he has fallen into the same destructive patterns yet again sounds like, "Listen, we *all* need rescue. Jesus said that *none* of us would make the cut if it weren't for him. I love you, man. Jesus loves you. How can I help you get connected to him?"

When our voices are reset for God's glory, the exchanges we have with people shift from being *transactional* to being *transformational*. Instead of using the three or four minutes we might have with someone we run into to talk about the weather, the results of the big game, how busy we are, our opinions on the latest presidential debate, what *she* said, or what *he* did, we ask God to help us invest that time in ways that will count—both in the moment and for eternity.

## OUR WORDS DRAW OUT POTENTIAL

Finally, the reset voice helps call out something beautiful in each struggling soul by reminding them who they are in Christ. When you and I internalize the scriptural truths that confirm our worth to Jesus, we start speaking those out to others who have been believing lies.

"You are loved."

"Jesus sees you."

"You are destined for great things."

"Jesus has amazing plans for your life."

"You were created on purpose, for a purpose."

"Jesus is committed to your wholeness."

These and tons of other truths can bring supernatural healing and hope to someone who is having a tough time in life. Remember, your words might be just the tool God will use to bring one who is languishing back to life. This really is how the world gets changed—one divinely encouraged heart at a time.

Can I give you one last tip? It's this: Develop the simple habit of calling on Jesus as often and as intentionally as you can. When something hard happens, cry out to Jesus. When someone needs advice, look to Jesus. When you drive, sit, work, exercise, and before you sleep, talk to Jesus.

Perhaps you're picking up on a theme here: *It's all about Jesus.*

## DISCUSS IT

*[Work through as many of the following questions as group time and interest will allow.]*

1. Based on what you typically talk about in everyday conversation, how would your acquaintances, friends, and family members describe you? The tech geek? The movie buff? The sports nut? The God girl? The talk-radio addict?

Someone else? Are you comfortable with this assessment? Why, or why not?

2. Think back on your own spiritual journey. Whose words did God use along the way to compel *you* to consider Jesus? A parent's words? A mentor's or friend's? A pastor's? Someone else's? Who spoke up, what did they say to you, and what was the effect on your life?

3. How often do you look for spiritual openings in conversations?

4. What fears or insecurities might keep you from speaking up on behalf of Jesus? What benefits might you know by doing so?

5. What current relationship of yours might serve as a logical place to experiment further with spiritual dialogue?

# THE INVITATION TO RESET

*[Allow time for your group to read the following invitation silently. Then, have a designated group member close your time in prayer.]*
If you are open to having Jesus reset your voice and are looking for a starting point, give this exercise a try: First, look back at the verses from pages 61 to 64 that you selected. Do you notice a theme among the ones you marked? Perhaps the common denominator is healing or strength, safety or forgiveness. Ask God to confirm the theme and then note it on the line below.

_____

Next, think about your answer to question 5 in the previous section. Is there an intersection between the theme you were drawn to and this person's current circumstances? For example, if you marked verses that seem to center on healing, and the person you noted in question 5 is your spouse, ask God to show you the connection between the two. In what ways is your spouse in need of healing? Is the healing spiritual in nature? Physical? Emotional? Something else?

Stay with the train of thought until you receive clarity on the matter. Then, ask God to give you the words to say to your spouse that will confirm in his or her heart that

Jesus stands ready to heal. Finally, find your spouse and *speak up*—which, admittedly, is the hardest part. But it's also the most awesome part, because as you acknowledge Jesus—his name, his power, his presence—in your relationships, you will experience a kind of joy that the world only *wishes* it could know.

Incidentally, this is the perfect time to point you toward a resource I've included at the back of this guide (on page 90), what I call the Keep5 prayer card. I've used this simple tool for fifteen years running as a way to list and pray for five people at a time in my life who are in need of the life-giving truth of Jesus. I jot down their names and I pray for them, both prayers of blessing over their lives and prayers of petition for God to give me opportunities to share Jesus with them. Based on the miracles that have unfolded in many of my Keep5 friends' lives, I have to believe God loves those kinds of prayers.

As you go about your days, keep those evidences of Jesus's power in mind. Ask God for open doors for sharing them (see Colossians 4:3). And then, as you're directed, *speak up.*

## CLOSING PRAYER

"Father, you say that as we are faithful to acknowledge Jesus before people, he will be faithful to acknowledge us before you. Please give us boldness as we communicate your truth and light to a world shrouded by darkness and lies. Reset our voices today, Father. We want to speak up for you. In Jesus's name, amen."

# WEEK 4

# "JESUS, RESET MY HANDS"

## SOUL AT PEACE, HANDS AT WORK

### KEY SCRIPTURE

*[Have someone in your group read these verses and the following Core Truth aloud before playing this week's video.]* "You, my brothers and sisters, were called to be free. But do not use your freedom to indulge the flesh; rather, serve one another humbly in love. For the entire law is fulfilled in keeping this one command: 'Love your neighbor as yourself.'" —Galatians 5:13–14

### CORE TRUTH

Once we are reset by Jesus, we get to join him in his work, which always involves freeing those in bondage, embracing those in isolation, and loving even the unlovely in our midst.

# VIDEO NOTES

*[Play this week's video and then take turns in your group reading the Study It paragraphs aloud.]*

## GALATIANS 5:13–14

_____

_____

_____

_____

_____

_____

_____

## PROGRAMMING OUR PRIORITIES

_____

_____

_____

_____

_____

_____

_____

## FOUR FRIENDS, ONE GOAL

_____

_____

_____

_____

_____

_____

_____

## FAITH THAT IMPRESSES EVEN JESUS

_____

_____

_____

_____

_____

_____

## WHAT YOU HAVE TO GIVE

_____

_____

_____

_____

_____

_____

# STUDY IT

For as long as I can remember, I've been a type-A kind of guy: sky-high energy; eternally optimistic; way too many balls being juggled at any given time; *push, push, push* for quicker decisions, more action, bigger opportunities, better results. Based on what my closest friends tell me, I can be a little . . . annoying. "Nick, just chill out, man," they implore me, even as my warrior brain is on to the next hill I'm determined to take.

Candidly, I would do well to listen to my friends' advice. I would do well to relax more than I do. But the thoughts that race through my mind every time I do try to unplug and veg out are that *life is short, time is ticking,* and *there is so much good work to be done.*

It took me a while to sort out what God's plan for my life was, so once I found it, I wanted to pursue it with everything I had—hence, my insatiable appetite for telling more and more people about Jesus and seeing their lives transformed just like mine. This week's passage (from Galatians 5) says that when we find freedom in Jesus, we should remember that freedom isn't just for our own benefit—as personally beneficial as it is!—but rather for the benefit of others too. In other words, once the shackles are removed from our own wrists, we are supposed to find people who are still bound up and work to set them free. My excuse, then, for overthinking, overplanning, overstrategizing, overworking, and over-everything-ing is that I am just wildly passionate about seeing others set free. (Or that's what I tell myself, anyway, when I'm overthinking why I overwork.)

## THE TWO PRACTICES

I tell you all of this by way of setup for this week's topic, which is how to translate our reset *faith* into reset *action*, a progression Scripture says will always be true of a true follower of Christ. (See James 2:17, 26.) The Bible teaches that there are two practices essential to the activation of our faith, and both practices are equally important. But just as I've disclosed to you in the previous section, I'm better at one of those practices than the other.

Here is the first practice: According to a whole slew of verses in God's Word, once we have embraced the message of Jesus and oriented our lives around his invitation of grace, we are to "go and share" that good news with other people. Let me show you a few passages that bear out this point:

- "Therefore go and make disciples of all nations, baptizing them in the name of the Father and of the Son and of the Holy Spirit." —Matthew 28:19

- "But you will receive power when the Holy Spirit comes on you; and you will be my witnesses in Jerusalem, and in all Judea and Samaria, and to the ends of the earth." —Acts 1:8

- "For, 'Everyone who calls on the name of the Lord will be saved.' How, then, can they call on the one they have not believed in? And how can they believe in the one of whom they have not heard? And how can they hear without someone preaching to them? And how can anyone preach unless they are sent? As it is written: 'How beautiful are the feet of those who bring good news!'" —Romans 10:13–15

- "What good is it, my brothers and sisters, if someone claims to have faith but has no deeds? Can such faith save them? Suppose a brother or a sister is without clothes and daily food. If one of you says to them, 'Go in peace; keep warm and well fed,' but does nothing about their physical needs, what good is it? In the same way, faith by itself, if it is not accompanied by action, is dead." —James 2:14–17

- "Carry each other's burdens, and in this way you will fulfill the law of Christ." —Galatians 6:2

- "'But a Samaritan, as he traveled, came where the man was; and when he saw him, he took pity on him. He went to him and bandaged his wounds, pouring on oil and wine. Then he put the man on his own donkey, brought him to an inn and took care of him. The next day he took out two denarii and gave them to the innkeeper. "Look after him," he said, "and when I return, I will reimburse you for any extra expense you may have." Which of these three do you think was a neighbor to the man who fell into the hands of robbers?' The expert in the law replied, 'The one who had mercy on him.' Jesus told him, 'Go and do likewise.'" —Luke 10:33–37

I love these verses. I love all the "go and do" words of encouragement you care to throw my way. Get up! Get going! Go do stuff in the name of Jesus! *Go, go, go! Do, do, do!* Now this is a practice I can totally get behind. This is where I really shine.

But "this" isn't the only practice involved. As I mentioned, there are *two*. And one is just as important as the other, remember? The practice that must accompany "going and doing"—that must *precede* it, in fact—is this: "Sit. And wait." *Sit and wait on the Lord.* And therein lies the rub—for me, anyway. (Can't I just go and do?)

## FIRST THINGS FIRST

It probably won't surprise you that there are just as many (maybe even more?) verses in Scripture that encourage sitting and waiting as those that say to go and do. Here are a few, just to substantiate the claim:

- "Trust in the LORD with all your heart and lean not on your own understanding; in all your ways submit to him, and he will make your paths straight." —Proverbs 3:5–6

- "The LORD will fight for you; you need only to be still." —Exodus 14:14

- "The LORD is in his holy temple; let all the earth be silent before him." —Habakkuk 2:20

- "But those who hope in the LORD will renew their strength. They will soar on wings like eagles; they will run and not grow weary, they will walk and not be faint." —Isaiah 40:31

- "Be patient, then, brothers and sisters, until the Lord's coming. See how the farmer waits for the land to yield its valuable crop, patiently waiting for the autumn and spring rains. You too, be patient and stand firm, because the Lord's coming is near." —James 5:7–8

- "The LORD is good to those whose hope is in him, to the one who seeks him." —Lamentations 3:25

- "But as for me, I watch in hope for the LORD, I wait for God my Savior; my God will hear me." —Micah 7:7

- "[The Lord] says, 'Be still, and know that I am God; I will be exalted among the nations, I will be exalted in the earth.'" —Psalm 46:10

God says that in our enthusiasm for taking the world *for* him—this is what reset faith compels us to do, after all—we must not forget that our strength is found only *in* him. And not just our strength, but also our creativity, our wisdom, our opportunities to do good, and more. We sit and wait on the Lord because it is in him that we are equipped to then go and do all the cool stuff he has for us to do.

## WORK THAT LIVES FOREVER

When we are faithful to (first!) sit and wait on instruction and direction from the Lord, and then to (second) go and do what he asks us to do, we can be sure that our efforts are "not in vain" (I Corinthians 15:58) and that we are on the exact path God has asked us to tread. Remember my friend from last week's session who took the job as a cook at the strip club in Fargo? Imagine if she had dreamed up that idea on her own instead of really seeking God's input: Her efforts would have most likely failed, and she may have been seduced into sinful behavior instead of being able to compel those living in darkness to consider choosing the light.

Similarly, the stories I mentioned in this week's video—of people I know who sold off possessions, sacrificed personal gain, risked ridicule and outright failure, and more, all for the sake of investing in kingdom work—all feature men and women who patiently sought the Lord before striking off in a given direction. They paused to pray, read Scripture, meditate on truth, and ask wise people if their plans might be "of God," and then—and *only* then—they put feet to their faith.

This is precisely why we have moved through the reset categories in the order that we have: because doing good in the name of God can really only happen as a result of a person's faith, mind, and voice being reset. Anything else is little more than a shortsighted strategy for selfish gain. But oh, the amazing adventures that unfold when we've patiently come before God—slowing our RPMs, banishing all our distractions, subduing our kill-it mode—and turned control back over to him. (It was his all along, you know.) We leave those times of deep intimacy with fresh awareness of his grace, fresh appreciation for his perspective, and fresh energy for joining him in his work. As we move through our day, watching for opportunities to speak a fitting word, to point a wayward soul toward him, to reach out to one who is marginalized, to drop someone an encouraging text, to pick up the tab for the harried mom in line behind us, to set aside our interests momentarily in favor of considering another's needs, we can be sure *God is directing our steps.*

# APPLY IT

*[Have one member of your group read the following section aloud as a prelude to the Discuss It questions.]*

Think critically about which of the two approaches comes more naturally for you—*sitting and waiting* or *going and doing*—and then consider these suggestions for shoring up the other one.

## SIT AND WAIT

We were made for intimate connection with Jesus, and that only comes by way of frequent, intentional, unrushed, undistracted encounters with him. If, like me, those adjectives make you jittery just reading them, let alone living them out, then give the following practices a try this week. (To the "go-happy" ones in the crowd, you're welcome.)

1. **Find a spot.** I have found that if I will simply designate a space in my house to spend time with God, I tend to be more faithful in meeting with him. Our house is overrun by toys at the moment, so my spot these days is a tiny corner of Tiffany's and my bedroom, but hey, whatever works. In that corner, I have a little nightstand with a Bible in the drawer. I have a journal there too and a pen, a candle, and also a lamp. Pick a place that will become holy ground, just by virtue of your meeting with Jesus there. And then go there first thing tomorrow.

2. **Set a timer.** Once you get to your spot, set the timer on your phone to alert you when fifteen minutes have passed. Instead of hoping for the Super Bowl of All Quiet Times right out of the gate, start small and see what unfolds.

3. **Declare it aloud.** This is a cool trick for you antsy types: Try spending the entire fifteen minutes speaking (or at least muttering) aloud. Open your Bible and read a passage of Scripture aloud. Then, tell God aloud what you notice in those verses: What's happening in them? Who is doing the action? What does that action have to do with you and your life today? Write down a useful thought in your journal, and then read that thought aloud to God. Close your time in prayer, telling him (aloud) how you feel about him, how you feel about the day you're heading into, and what character

traits you'd like more of as you work through whatever challenges you are facing. Speaking the full experience will help you stay focused, not on your dirty house, your massive to-do list, or your Instagram account but on *God*. Novel idea, right?

Before you know it, fifteen minutes will have elapsed, and you'll be reaping all the unparalleled benefits of spending time with God: inner peace, sure confidence, deep-seated joy, and that certain radiance people possess when they've been in the presence of the divine. Bring it, God!

## GO AND DO

Despite the fact that I don't fall into this category, I have noticed a trend among some believers, which is that they love the "sitting and waiting" part at the exclusion of all "going and doing." (I think we call these "holy huddles," yes?) They enjoy studying, reading, analyzing, learning, worshipping, praying, and *thinking, thinking, thinking,* but when it comes to actually *activating* their faith, they shy away. The darkness in the world is so *dark*. The sins are so *sinful*. The pain is so *painful*. The struggles are so *real*.

People are so . . . messy, and these sitters/waiters want to stay neat. Plus it feels pretty good to just talk about, spend time with, and think about Jesus.

If you fall into this category, allow me to encourage you with this: You would not be sitting here, enjoying the peace and joy of Christ-followership, if someone had not "gone and done" for you. Remember that verse from Romans 10 we looked at earlier? It posed the question, "But how can people call for help if they don't know who to trust? And how can they know who to trust if they haven't heard of the One who can be trusted? And how can they hear if nobody tells them?" (verse 14, MSG). At some point, it's not enough to rest in the life we have found in Jesus; we must take that life to those who are dying inside. Besides, how can we say we are following Jesus if we never do the things he did? If you say you want to be like LeBron James yet you never set foot in the gym, reasonable people would call your bluff.

Here again, it pays to start small. Tomorrow as you go about your day, ask God periodically for his input. For example, If you're in a conversation with someone, ask, "God, what are you up to in this person's life? Are you speaking to them? What are you hoping to see in their life?" If he prompts you to say something encouraging, or to offer up a resource of some kind, *do it*. Don't hesitate, overanalyze, or shy away. Just go for it. In the name of Jesus, go for it.

Often, it's not that we lack knowledge of God's promptings; we just lack the courage to carry them out. As you are led to say and do loving, thoughtful, sacrificial, unselfish things, *do them,* resting assured that the leadings are from God. Because really, who among us dreams up ways to be unselfish on our own? No, every good and perfect others-focused idea is God's, and God's alone. Get into the habit of asking him what he's up to—in this person's heart, in that situation, in this headline, in that meeting, in this neighborhood, in that relationship, in this goal, in that challenge—and then join him, right where he is. And if you have to err, err on the side of doing. I have yet to hear someone say they really blew it by sharing Jesus's love with someone.

Your to-do lists and errands, your shareholder meetings and strategy offsites, your late-night study sessions and final exams—all the Very Important Work we're so busy doing—will one day return to dust. But *this* work, the work of pointing people to Jesus by our faith, our presence, our love? This is the work of *eternal* consequence. This work will never die.

## DISCUSS IT

*[Work through as many of the following questions as group time and interest will allow.]*

1. Would you say that you're more likely to "sit and wait" or to "go and do"? What advantages and disadvantages to your approach have you discovered firsthand?

2. What fears, frustrations, insecurities, or obstacles keep you from more faithfully practicing the other discipline?

3. What excites you about becoming more balanced in your approach to reaching this generation for Jesus?

4. Who in your relational circle practices the other discipline well and might be willing to swap helpful suggestions with you and hold you accountable as you work to follow both of God's mandates here—that we become disciplined in seeking his guidance and also bold in declaring our faith?

# THE INVITATION TO RESET

*[Allow time for your group to read the following invitation silently. Then, have a designated group member close your time in prayer.]*
If you are ready for a reset of how your faith gets translated into action—a "reset of the hands," if you will—then spend a few minutes considering our mission as lovers of God, as relayed in the story mentioned in this week's video.

> *A few days later, when Jesus again entered*
> *Capernaum, the people heard that he had*
> *come home. They gathered in such large*
> *numbers that there was no room left, not*
> *even outside the door, and he preached the*
> *word to them. Some men came, bringing*
> *to him a paralyzed man, carried by four*
> *of them. Since they could not get him to*

*Jesus because of the crowd, they made an*

*opening in the roof above Jesus by digging*

*through it and then lowered the mat the*

*man was lying on. When Jesus saw their*

*faith, he said to the paralyzed man, "Son,*

*your sins are forgiven."*

*Now some teachers of the law were*

*sitting there, thinking to themselves,*

*"Why does this fellow talk like that? He's*

*blaspheming! Who can forgive sins but*

*God alone?"*

*Immediately Jesus knew in his spirit*

*that this was what they were thinking in*

*their hearts, and he said to them, "Why*

*are you thinking these things? Which is eas-*

*ier: to say to this paralyzed man, 'Your sins*

*are forgiven,' or to say, 'Get up, take your*

*mat and walk'? But I want you to know*

*that the Son of Man has authority on earth*

*to forgive sins." So he said to the man, "I*

*tell you, get up, take your mat and go*

*home." He got up, took his mat and walked*

*out in full view of them all. This amazed*

*everyone and they praised God, saying,*

*"We have never seen anything like this!"*

*(Mark 2:1–12)*

Don't miss this! Every time we are faithful to act on a quietly whispered, divinely inspired prompting to set aside self-focused concerns, to show hospitality, to speak kindly, to serve well, and to love well, we are—in the same way that these four friends got their buddy to Jesus as fast as they could—"getting someone to Jesus." And why wouldn't we want to be part of this eternal transformation?

We get people to Jesus because in him healing is found.

We get people to Jesus because in him fulfillment is found.

We get people to Jesus because in him freedom is found.

We get people to Jesus because we recognize that no one and nothing else can solve the problems that distance from him creates.

Ultimately, we get people to Jesus because he alone is the one with the power to declare inside-out restoration over every troubled soul the world has ever known: "Your sins are forgiven! Now, get up and walk."

## CLOSING PRAYER

"Father, give us patience to sit and wait on you. And give us boldness to act on what we learn in the waiting. In Jesus's name we pray, amen."

# KEEP5

"I pray that you may be active in sharing your faith, so that you will have a full understanding of every good thing we have in Christ." – PHILEMON 1:6

## I WILL

- WRITE down the names of five people who need Jesus,
- PRAY for them every day, and
- LOOK for opportunities to share Jesus with them.

1 _____

2 _____

3 _____

4 _____

5 _____

When we pray, Jesus moves!

» PULSE

PULSEMOVEMENT.COM

# NOTES

## WEEK 1: "JESUS, RESET MY HEART"

1 Nick Hall, *Reset: Jesus Changes Everything* (Colorado Springs, CO: Multnomah, 2016), 59.

2 *Reset*, 60.

3 *Reset*, 62–63.

4 *Reset*, 123.

## WEEK 2: "JESUS, RESET MY MIND"

1 Nick Hall, *Reset: Jesus Changes Everything* (Colorado Springs, CO: Multnomah, 2016), 95.

2 Sheree Johnson, "New Research Sheds Light on Daily Ad Exposures," SJ Insights, September 29, 2014, http://sjinsights .net/2014/09/29/new-research-sheds-light-on-daily-ad-exposures from *Reset*, 141.

3 M. Dittmann, "Self-esteem that's based on external sources has mental health consequences, study says," *Monitor on Psychology*, December 2002, Vol 33, No. 11, p. 16, http://www.apa .org/monitor/dec02/selfesteem.aspx.

4 "Self-acceptance could be the key to a happier life, yet it's the happy habit many people practice the least," *ScienceDaily*, March 7, 2014, http://www.sciencedaily.com/releases /2014/03/140307111016.htm.

5 "Self-acceptance."

6 Alec Gallup and Wendy W. Simmons, "Six in Ten Americans Read Bible at Least Occasionally," October 20, 2000, http:// www.gallup.com/poll/2416/six-ten-americans-read-bible-least-occasionally.aspx.

7 "American Bible Society's State of the Bible 2015," http://www .americanbible.org/features/state-of-the-bible-2015.

8 Samantha Grossman, "On a Daily Basis, Americans Read Facebook More Than the Bible," *Time*, February 5, 2014, http:// time.com/4561/americans-read-facebook-more-than-the-bible/.

9 *Reset*, 91.

# ABOUT THE AUTHOR

Nick Hall didn't set out to found PULSE, he set out to share the hope of Jesus on his college campus—and so many people's lives were impacted that PULSE was founded to help keep the message spreading.

As a voice to the next generation, Nick has shared the message of Jesus at hundreds of events to millions of students and is regularly featured as a speaker for pastors' gatherings, student conferences, training events, and festivals around the world. He has a passion for student-led prayer movements, leadership training, evangelism, and discipleship and has received hands-on training from some of the most influential Christian leaders of our day. He sits on the leadership teams for the US Lausanne Committee, the National Association of Evangelicals, and the student advisory team for the Billy Graham Evangelistic Association (BGEA) and is a partner evangelist with the Luis Palau Association. In the spring of 2011, he was welcomed to the National Facilitation Committee for the Mission America Coalition (MAC). Nick has a bachelor's degree in Business Administration from North Dakota State University and a master's in Leadership and Christian Thought from Bethel Seminary in St. Paul, Minnesota. Nick and his wife, Tiffany, have two children and live in Minneapolis, Minnesota.